TYRONE GORDON

AFRICAN AMERICAN HISTORY MONTH 2012

Daily Devotions

ABINGDON PRESS / NASHVILLE

African American History Month Daily Devotions, 2012

Introduction

This devotional is designed to celebrate a rich history, a deep sense of spirituality, and a commitment to the pursuit of justice and righteousness in the world during African American History Month 2012. This devotional comes out of my spiritual DNA that helped me understand that the God of my elders was and is a relevant and contemporary source of strength for my survival today. Some of the passages of Scripture are familiar, some are meant to challenge us to keep fighting the good fight of faith for justice, and some might be obscure but will inspire you to become all God has created you to be.

I pray that this devotional during this month that has been set aside to commemorate the contributions of African Americans will be a helpful tool. Not only will it help you recall history but it will also help you remember that spirituality was a great part of that history. It was those ancestors who taught so many of us that God is able. May this devotion help you begin, end, or just get through each day being reminded by faith that God is able. Be blessed in your walk with the Lord.

I must thank God and my family. To my beautiful wife, Marsha; and my daughters Lauren and Allyson—thank you for your support and love. To my mother, Mrs. Jean Gordon Smith; my nana, Mrs. O.V. Smith; and my sister, Cynthia Gordon Martin—you all laid the foundation in my life. I am because you are. I love you all so very much. To my staff and members of St. Luke, with special kudos to my administrative assistant, Ms. Carolyn Howard—many thanks for your love and support. To my prayer partners, encouragers, and brothers too numerous to list—thank you for your prayers.

Tyrone D. Gordon

And the Struggle Continues . . .

Read Ephesians 6:10-17.

We aren't fighting against human enemies but against rulers, authorities, forces of cosmic darkness, and spiritual powers of evil in the heavens.
(Ephesians 6:12)

Coming on the heels of our celebration of the life and ministry of Dr. Martin Luther King Jr., and the beginning of the commemoration of Black History Month, we must be reminded that the struggle continues. Dr. Zan Holmes is fond of saying, "Nothing stays won." We are in the midst of an age-old struggle, a hostile conflict between good and evil, love and hate, war and peace, acceptance and intolerance, justice and injustice, righteousness and unrighteousness, God and Satan.

This is an intense spiritual battle with social implications. There is a demonic assault on your possibilities, opportunities, gifts, and talents. Any attack on our human dignity and rights is demonic and must be confronted with the power of heaven. Every day we must prepare to face attacks on our mental stability, our spiritual sanity, and our social responsibility by ensuring that we are clothed in the whole armor of God. As you move about today, decide right now that you are a survivor. You are more than a conqueror.

I remember a little praise song we used to sing: "I went to the enemies' camp and I took back what was stolen from me." Live today with a take-back spirit. We're taking back our children. We're taking back our communities. We're taking back our peace. We're taking back our financial security. We're taking back our joy. We're taking it all back. It will be a struggle, but we are in a winnable battle. For Jesus says in John 10:10, "The thief enters only to steal, kill, and destroy. I came so that they could have life—indeed, so that they could live life to the fullest."

Prayer: God, give us a spirit that is not afraid to be in the struggle for justice, peace, and righteousness. Help us continue to fight the good fight of faith. In Jesus' name. Amen.

Don't Give Up Too Soon

Read Luke 5:1-11.

Simon replied, "Master, we've worked hard all night and caught nothing. But because you say so, I'll drop the nets." (Luke 5:5)

Resilience, faith, persistence, and determination are characteristics of a people who have been to hell and back and lived to tell their story. These are characteristics of a people who know what it means to be locked out, locked down, and locked up, but keep pressing on anyhow. It's a part of the DNA of people who always find a way to survive and thrive when the odds are stacked against them.

Peter and his colleagues had been fishing all night and came up empty, frustrated, and tired. All they had to show for their efforts were empty nets. They were about to call it quits. They were about to bring things to a close and wrap it up when Jesus showed up and suggested that they keep at it just a little longer and go out a little deeper. Peter's response to Jesus' challenge has always caught my attention: "Master, we've worked hard all night and caught nothing. But because you say so, I'll drop the nets."

The Lord's advice stretched them beyond their limits. Sometimes in our weariness, despondency, and frustration we want to throw in the towel and call it quits. But the Lord's word for us today is "don't give up too soon." Don't close the doors on your possibilities. Don't allow the failures of your past to prevent you from experiencing the new opportunities of the future. Like Peter, be willing to make the adjustments to do what needs to be done to move forward with your life.

I don't know where you are in life, in ministry, in your relationships, or your career, but don't miss your appointment with destiny by giving up too soon. The Lord is always up to something. When we least expect it, the Lord seems to always show up to encourage us, strengthen us, and move us to the next level in our lives.

Prayer: O Lord, give me the strength and fortitude to keep pushing forward when life knocks me back. Give me today a determination that will not allow me to give up too soon. In Jesus' name. Amen.

Get Your Feet Wet

Read Joshua 3:7-17.

"The soles of the priests' feet, who are carrying the chest of the LORD, ruler of the whole earth, will come to rest in the water of the Jordan. At that moment, the water of the Jordan will be cut off. The water flowing downstream will stand still in a single heap." (Joshua 3:13)

This is a story of new beginnings and transition. Forty years had passed and a new day with a new generation had come to the threshold of a new future. They were excited and anxious about entering the Promised Land, but as life would have it, a barrier stood in the way; it stood between them and the future; it stood between them and the promise. In order to get what they wanted, they had to move ahead, and that would require that they get their feet wet.

We can't go through life standing on the edge of the promise—it is time to move into the promise. However, I know that we can become comfortable with the status quo and let fear keep us from moving on, moving out, and moving up. We can get used to some unholy and unhealthy things in order to hold on to the familiar: unhealthy relationships, unhealthy people, unhealthy friendships, unhealthy surroundings. In order to break free and move forward, we are going to have to face those swollen, overflowing rivers by getting our feet wet.

Moving into new territory is always a risky venture of faith. But we should never underestimate the power and role faith plays in the plans of God. Faith empowers us and it gets God's attention. The river backed up when the priests stepped into the waters. It took a miracle; it took God's intervention to make the crossing of the river possible. It would have never been experienced without an act of faith.

Today, make a determination that you refuse to hang out on the water's edge of the promise but are willing to risk getting your feet wet to move toward a new day and new beginnings.

Prayer: Lord, today I resolve to get my feet wet and march into a new future, trusting in your Word and standing on your promises. Help me trust you in everything this day. In Jesus' name. Amen.

Remembering Those Who Paved the Way

Read Joshua 4:1-9.

"In the future your children may ask, 'What do these stones mean to you?' Then you will tell them that the water of the Jordan was cut off before the LORD's covenant chest. When it crossed over the Jordan, the water of the Jordan was cut off. These stones will be an enduring memorial for the Israelites." (Joshua 4:6b-7)

For me, black history cannot be contained in and celebrated just one month a year. All the contributions African Americans have made to our society cannot be contained in the shortest and coldest month of the year. There are too many persons to remember, too many deeds to celebrate, too many to pay homage to and remember who paved our way. We should never become so arrogant that we forget from where we've come and who helped us get here.

We are to hold our elders in regard and respect because of the price they paid for us. We are here because somebody struggled. Somebody fought. Somebody went the extra mile. Somebody was beaten. Somebody sat in. Somebody was the first. The problem with many of us who are living in the post–civil rights era is that we often think that the way things are is the way it has always been. Not so! Somebody paved the way. Joshua commanded the people, after their miraculous crossing of the Jordan, to build a memorial so that future generations had an understanding of how they got to where they were.

We owe a great debt to the elders who paved the way. When I look at my still-active grandmother, who got her driver's license renewed for five years on her ninety-seventh birthday, I can't help telling God, "Thank you for those who paved the way." They taught us how to survive, thrive, and be who God created us to be. They taught us God could open doors, make ways out of no ways, and fight our battles if we keep still. Thank God for their witness, their sacrifices, their strength, their work, their struggles, and their prayers.

Prayer: O God, thank you for the elders who nurtured us, taught us, and instilled in us our faith. They went through so we could get through. Thank you, God, for those who paved the way. Amen.

When God Puts Us on Hold

Read Job 23:1-10.

*Surely he knows my way; when he tests me, I will
emerge as gold. (Job 23:10)*

Many of us can relate to the story of Job. We learn quickly how fickle life, people, and circumstances can be. Job's emotional and spiritual life swung like a pendulum from one end of the spectrum to another. He swung from confidence to uncertainty, from understanding to anger, from peace to confusion, from faith to doubt, from praise to bitterness, from strength to weakness, and from joy to sorrow. After losing everything he held dear and precious, he felt as if God had put his whole life on hold. Feelings of abandonment, alienation, punishment, and loneliness filled his mind. Have you ever been there?

We've all been there. We've all been at a place where we felt that our lives, our destinies, and our opportunities were all put on hold. Everything was off-center and our focus skewed. Life tore up. Relationships jacked up. Mind messed up. Dreams broken up. Future locked. Faith shaken up. Bills stacked up. Money dried up. And we were emotionally held up. Everything was at a standstill and we felt as if God had placed us on hold. But in those moments I refused to give up. It was time to look up. Experience has taught me the harder the trial, the greater the coming blessing.

In my travels, there have been times my flight has been put in a holding pattern. We were en route but we could not land at that time. Being placed in a divine holding pattern does not mean the flight to our destiny has been canceled; it simply means we're not ready to land or it's not safe to land. A dream deferred is not a dream denied. It's in our holding pattern that God is working in our lives, our situations, in our environment, and on us. God puts us on hold, not to keep us from our destination but to ensure we get to our destination safe and sound.

Prayer: Lord, strengthen our determination, knowing that what you started in us, you will bring out of us. Help us to have patience to wait until our change comes.

Divine Troublemakers

Read 1 Kings 18:16-19.

*When Ahab saw Elijah, Ahab said to him, "Is that you,
the one who troubles Israel?" (1 Kings 18:17)*

When visiting the new Martin Luther King Jr. Memorial in Washington, D.C., I was in awe as I recalled how God used him and the other freedom fighters of the civil rights movement. Time has sanitized his memory as it has that of Jesus of Nazareth. Yet there is one thing we must admit about Dr. King and Jesus: they were both divine troublemakers. They were rebels, radicals, dissenters, revolutionaries, and agitators. They dared to challenge their people and nation to live up to God's standards and down to theirs.

In this day and time, we need more divine troublemakers, those voices of righteousness and justice who are not afraid to declare in a sin-torn society God's will and God's Word. The church is at her best when she becomes the conscience of the day, challenging the status quo and not simply going with the flow. She is the one who troubles the waters of complacency, mediocrity, injustice, war, poverty, racism, sexism, and any other "isms" that keep all of God's children from living up to their created potential.

Elijah was that troublemaker for Ahab and Jezebel's government. He was a threat to the practices of a nation, which lived like they lost their minds and forgot the One who brought them out of Egypt. Elijah was a menace to a society that exploited and ignored the most vulnerable in it and turned its back on the most needy. Ahab was so intimidated by the prophet that he changed his appointment calendar to meet him. The first thing out of his mouth was, "Is that you, the one who troubles Israel?"

Let's commit today to be God's divine troublemakers until hatred turns into love, war into peace, darkness into light, and God makes all things new.

Prayer: Here we are, Lord. Use us today to disturb and trouble the waters of things that are not like you. In Your name do we pray. Amen.

There's Been a Change in Plans

Read Acts 11:1-18.

"If God gave them the same gift he gave us who believed in the Lord Jesus Christ, then who am I? Could I stand in God's way?" (Acts 11:17)

Have you ever had things laid out, mapped out, and strategically planned out only to have an unexpected change in your plans? To be honest, we don't like anything or anyone interfering with our plans. We don't like glitches, interruptions, or any tampering with our traditions, habits, and routines, especially in the church. Yet God is constantly on the move and keeps stretching us as God is always doing a new thing in our lives, our world, and in the church. If God never nudged us into a new future, we would get really comfortable with where we are and what we've done. God has a way of disrupting our routines, our way of thinking, and our way of doing things to announce "there has been a change in plans!"

The early church had to be called on the carpet for its prejudices, discriminatory practices, and arrogance. With the conversion of Cornelius and other Gentiles, the church had to rethink its theology. Peter's vision was God's challenge to open the doors of the church to all peoples. Of course there was a great church controversy behind all of this. Change always brings conflict, resistance, and rebellion. Thank God for God's changes down through history.

Had God not interrupted and intervened in history, there would have been no Harriet Tubman and the Underground Railroad. There would have been no Nat Turner, who refused to be a slave and fought for freedom. There would have been no Rosa Parks, whose courage caused her to sit down so that we could stand up. There would have been no Martin Luther King Jr., Archbishop Desmond Tutu, Nelson Mandela, Oprah Winfrey, Colin Powell, Condoleezza Rice, or Barack Obama. God will interrupt and intervene to declare that there has been a change in plans. God's intrusion into our social, spiritual, and cultural systems will cause us to rethink how we see others who are different from us.

Prayer: Lord, help us become a part of your new thing, your change of our plans. In Jesus' name. Amen.

This Is Not What I Planned

Read Luke 1:26-28.

Then Mary said, "I am the Lord's servant. Let it be with me just as you have said." Then the angel left her. (Luke 1:38)

Mary's encounter with the angel Gabriel totally and radically changed her life and her plans. On the heels of her arranged marriage, God barged in and informed her that there had been a dramatic change in plans. I can imagine a puzzled look on Mary's face that said it all: "This is not what I planned."

In these tough economic times, people all over are experiencing changes that were not in their plans. Sometimes our best-laid plans can suddenly be canceled, altered, or changed because God has other plans. God might be working in your life in ways you have never experienced; God might be pulling at your mind to go in directions you had not intended because it was not what you had planned. It might not have been in your plans but it was a part of God's plans since the foundation of the world. The issue here is that God sees things in you that you may not see in yourself. Once God puts the plans in motion, no power in heaven, on earth, or in hell can stop them.

What God was doing in Mary's life had dramatic implications; in fact, it was a recipe for social and religious disaster. You know that Mary's being unmarried and pregnant was a juicy church scandal, and fodder for church gossip at its best. When God alters our plans, we can be assured God has everything worked out. While we are baffled at the ways of God, God knows the way the God is taking us. Because with God, nothing will be impossible. It may not have been what we planned but it's a part of God's plans and the only thing we can say is yes. Yes to God's way and yes to God's will. Today, just say yes.

Prayer: Lord, help us say yes to your diverting of our plans. Help us see what you are doing and where you are going, and we say let it be done to us according to your word. In Jesus' name. Amen.

But if Not . . .

Read Daniel 3:13-18.

"If our God whom we serve is able to deliver us from the furnace of blazing fire and out of your hand, O king, let him deliver us. But if not, be it known to you, O king, that we will not serve your gods and we will not worship the golden statue that you have set up." (Daniel 3:17-18 NRSV)

What happens when we pray, have faith, and believe, but the outcome is not what we had envisioned? What happens when the healing does not materialize? The cancer is no longer in remission? The HIV has turned into full-blown AIDS? The layoff notice has been received? Death has taken a loved one? The mountain does not move? The answer is not what we wanted? What is the response when deliverance does not come, miracles are scarce, and blessings are nominal? Can our faith survive through those "but if not" moments?

Shadrach, Meshach, and Abednego had enough faith, commitment, and strength to survive their "but if not" moments. In the midst of overwhelming opposition, they refused the pressure to bow down and renounce their faith, identity, community, or God. Against threat after threat, these three were unmoved and unafraid because God had not given them a spirit of fear. They knew God was able and God could deliver, but if deliverance did not come, they still would not bow.

We all must know how to handle those "but if not" moments. It takes a radical faith that dares to risk, that gets us through those times in life. A "but if not" faith still trusts and believes even if the outcome may not be favorable. Those three never questioned God's ability but stood firm in their convictions based on principles and not just miracles. It's an "I still believe" faith. If God does not heal, we still believe. If we have to go through the fire, we still believe. If things don't end up the way we planned, we still believe. Our God is able to deliver, but if not, we still won't bow, break, or give in.

Prayer: God, help us stand for the sake of standing, not for the benefit of the miracle. Help us stand on principle, convictions, justice, and faith, knowing you are able to deliver. But if you don't, we still won't bow.

It All Begins with a Dream

Read Genesis 37:1-11, 17-20.

"The brothers said to each other, 'Here comes the big dreamer.' " (Genesis 37:19)

My favorite Scripture is Jeremiah 29:11: " 'For I know the plans I have for you,' declares the LORD, 'plans to prosper you and not to harm you, plans to give you hope and a future' " (NRSV). Those plans begin to unfold as God places the dreams of our destiny in our hearts. Everybody ought to have a dream, a vision that is not yet, but can be through the power of God at work in our lives. Dreams are God-inspired ideas that have been planted in our minds and spirits that speak to our future, our purpose, and our destiny. They permit us to imagine great and new possibilities of what we can do and accomplish.

Joseph began to have dreams at the age of seventeen, dreams of his future, dreams that gave him drive, focus, and purpose. His brothers were jealous and envious of their brother who dared to buck the status quo and dream big dreams for God. Everyone may not be able to handle the dreams God has placed in your spirit, so guard them with your life.

God is preparing you, even now, and getting you ready for your appointment with destiny. However, fulfilling these dreams and living into our future will not take place without our going through inevitable challenges and overcoming many barriers, as did Joseph. Don't let criticism, uncertainties, financial upheaval, delayed timelines, detours, small-minded people, or jealousy destroy your God-given dreams. Stay focused. Stay faithful. Just remember, God is the fuel and energy behind your dreams and no one can stop what God has started. It will be an uphill journey and it will be a challenging walk of faith. The dream may be delayed but it will not be denied.

Prayer: Lord, fill our hearts and minds with your dreams for our lives, our world, our churches, and our communities. Thank you for taking us places we know not of. As you lead, we will follow. In Jesus' name. Amen.

Grudges Can Be Deadly

Read Genesis 50:15-21.

"You planned something bad for me, but God produced something good from it, in order to save the lives of many people, just as he's doing today."
(Genesis 50:20)

We know how to hold grudges. We can stay mad a long time even after we have forgotten what started the conflict in the first place. To be truthful, forgiveness is hard, even for the most committed of Christians. It is a process that takes time, hard work, much prayer, determination, and sometimes counseling. But with the help of God, it can be done. Unresolved conflict can affect every area of our lives and every relationship we touch. It destroys us emotionally, mentally, physically, and spiritually. We go through life with chips on our shoulders, attitudes like none other, and a disposition that has been soaked in vinegar. Grudges have disrupted friendships, busted relationships, splintered churches, strained marriages, and wreaked havoc on families. Grudges can be deadly.

Joseph had every right to hold a grudge against his brothers. Their jealousy made his life a living hell when they sold him into slavery, killing his dreams, squashing his destiny, and destroying his spirit. But Joseph must have learned somewhere along the way that resentment imprisons us while forgiveness frees us. He teaches us that forgiveness is a choice.

Forgiveness is a liberating experience. It gives us power and freedom over the offender and the offense and opens the doors to experience reconciliation. When my younger brother was murdered in the streets of Los Angeles, I had a hard time forgiving. It took time but I soon discovered holding on to the negative energy of a grudge was doing more harm to me than to those who committed the offense. When I let go of the hatred, I experienced new life. Learn to let go of the hurt. Let go of the pain. Let go of the resentment. Let go of the grudge and watch God flip the script. What was meant for evil, God will turn into good.

Prayer: Lord, if I've wounded anyone today, help me seek forgiveness. If I've been wounded today, help me let go of the grudge. In Jesus' name do I pray. Amen.

Still Standing

Read 2 Corinthians 4:7-12.

We who are alive are always being handed over to death for Jesus' sake so that Jesus' life can also be seen in our bodies that are dying.
(2 Corinthians 4:11)

We all have a story. We all even have a story behind that story. Historically, personally, spiritually, mentally, and socially, our souls can still look back and wonder, *How in the world did we get over?* Nothing in life, in our experiences, or in history was able to deliver that fatal blow to take us out, take us down, or take us under. At our disposal have always been the inexhaustible resources of God, which have the ability to turn potential victims into faith-filled, still-standing victors. Instead of becoming a statistic, we have a testimony because, after all we've been through, we can say, "I'm still standing."

In my childhood one of my favorite toys was a punching bag in the image of Bozo the Clown. It fascinated me. Every time I hit it, it would go down and then bounce back up. No matter how hard I hit it, it bounced back up. You may have taken some hits, or might currently be taking some hard hits emotionally, economically, mentally, and socially, but you have something deep inside of you that gives you the power to bounce back.

All the rumors of your demise have been greatly exaggerated because you are still standing. When the dust clears and mess settles, you are still standing. Still standing after overwhelming tragedies. Still standing after life's dramatic changes. Still standing after layoffs and unemployment. Still standing after betrayal. Still standing after life-altering transitions. You are still standing. In fact, like the Apostle Paul, our testimony is "We are experiencing all kinds of trouble, but we aren't crushed. We are confused, but we aren't depressed. We are harassed, but we aren't abandoned. We are knocked down, but we aren't knocked out" (2 Corinthians 4:8-9).

Prayer: Lord, thank you for the power of the resurrection that is at work within us. Praise the power of your name. Amen.

You're on the List

Read Matthew 26:20-30.

> *As they were eating he said, "I assure you that*
> *one of you will betray me." (Matthew 26:21)*

If anyone historically knows what it's like to be left out and on the fringe, it's African Americans. Jim Crow, segregation, and legal discrimination tried to keep us off the list, but the Lord opened doors that were once closed to us. The table of the Lord was a place where he practiced inclusion and not exclusion. Knowing what the Lord knew, he kept everyone at that table on the list of invited guests. One would betray him, another would deny him, and the others would desert him. But they were still on the list.

Some years ago, when I was serving a church in Wichita, Kansas, I had the opportunity to serve as an elected president of the board of education. Some of the established political leaders and movers and shakers in the community thought I climbed too fast into political influence without paying the dues. President Bill Clinton was coming to town and somehow I was not on the list of invited guests to meet him, even though I was an elected official and the pastor of one of the largest African American churches in town. I had been snubbed.

I called a good pastor friend of mine in Arkansas whose brother-in-law happened to be in President Clinton's Cabinet. Shortly, I received a call from the White House telling me where to catch the shuttle. When I stepped on the bus, the others looked at me strangely and asked, "Whose guest are you?" I simply replied, "The White House." When we arrived, a guard asked if Tyrone Gordon was on the bus. I responded yes. He said, "Follow me, you're on my list."

You are on God's list regardless of what others think or what you've done. The invitation is "Come on over here where the table is spread and the feast of the Lord is going on."

Prayer: Lord, thank you for putting us on the list when others discounted us and blocked us. Thank you for your inclusion when we've experienced exclusion. In the accepting name of Jesus our Christ. Amen.

What's Love Got to Do with It?

Read John 13:31-35.

"This is how everyone will know that you are my disciples,
when you love each other." (John 13:35)

Sunday dinner after church was always big, special, and delicious, like what we would see on the end credits of the movie *Soul Food.* It was off the chain. Some of life's most profound, inspirational, and transformational conversations take place around the dinner table. Jesus engages his disciples in some holy table talk during his last meal with them. This talk prepared them for things to come and gave them the marks and fruits that true disciples of his should have. He left at the table his expectations of how they and we are to act toward one another. We are to love radically, unconditionally, and sacrificially.

I know wheels are spinning and our excuses are already formulating. The excuse I always hear is "Pastor, this is easier said than done." However, I do not believe that Jesus would require us to do anything that through the Holy Spirit we could not be empowered to accomplish. For Jesus, loving one another is nonnegotiable. Like his disciples, we all come with our differences, our quirks, our attitudes, our strengths, our weaknesses, our diversity, and our varied theological perspectives; but the link between us would be the love, the loyalty, the respect, the dignity, and the goodwill we will have for one another. Like the disciples, we don't all have to agree, but we are unified in our love for Christ and one another.

Jesus expects us to make a statement to the world, not by our words but by our actions. The thread that holds us all together is the love we have for one another, as Christ has loved us. This is what a divided and hateful world needs to witness. By this, everyone will know that we are God's disciples, if we love one another. Love has everything to do with it.

Prayer: Dear Lord, may I be a witness to your love in a world divided by political ideologies, race, and national origin. May others say "There goes one of God's disciples" when they see and feel the love. In your name. Amen.

FEBRUARY 15

Built Not to Break

Read Isaiah 40:28-31.

His understanding is beyond human reach, giving power to the tired and reviving the exhausted. *(Isaiah 40:28b-29)*

W e're built strong, sturdy, and secure; in fact, we were built not to break. That's good news because the times in which we live, the losses we have suffered, and the breakups we've endured could have snapped us in two. But the power that is at work within us kept us from crumbling, buckling, collapsing, and breaking down. We were not built to break.

This passage of Scripture has been a source of encouragement, strength, and inspiration down through the centuries. It reminds us that when we are at our weakest, God is at God's strongest. What we lack, God will supply. We were built to last, to endure and not break. We have to teach ourselves to bend with adversity and not break from it.

We have the secret of resilience as we are plugged into the inexhaustible resources of God. It's as if we need the assurance from God to keep us, sustain us, and cover us in times of great stress and struggle. Circumstances, experiences, and people can stab us in the heart, wound our spirits, and lash out at us with every intention of bringing us down and taking us out, but fortunately, we were built not to break. There will be days when life will be brutally hard, painfully difficult, and crushingly overwhelming. In the midst of it all, we can look at ourselves knowing that what should have taken us out instead made us stronger, more courageous, and determined. It's as if something inside tells us, "Let the vise tighten, let the attacks come, but when the dust settles and the view clears we will see we were built not to break." We might crash, we might tumble, but thank God we won't crumble. Because of the power that is at work within us, we were built not to break.

Prayer: O God, thank you for your undergirding power and strength that keeps us in our most difficult times and challenges. Thank you that in your infinite wisdom we are built not to break. In Jesus' name. Amen.

Come Out of Hiding

Read Genesis 3:8-13.

**"The LORD God called to the man [Adam] and said to him,
"Where are you?" (Genesis 3:9)**

As we commemorate Black History Month, I would be remiss if I didn't have a word for our brothers. Many are well aware of the statistics and issues of being a black male in America. But God still has a word of hope and challenge to African American brothers. God wants us to come out of hiding. God came to the garden of Eden in the cool of the evening for the daily interactions with Adam, but for the first time, Adam could not be found. He was AWOL because of his disobedience to God. He was on the run, driven by his fears, his shame, and his guilt. God's question is still relevant in 2012: "Adam, where are you?"

God calls out to us so that we can face up to some things, let our guard down and be transparent before our God. Adam was in hiding because he believed the lies of the enemies of life, joy, and peace. Remember God's famous question to Adam, "Who told you that you were naked?" We've been handicapped, debilitated, and devastated. That is why so many black men have been in hiding. Who fed us the lies of what we couldn't do and couldn't be? Who told us we could not survive? Who told us we could not excel? Who told us we would never amount to much? Who told us we could only excel in sports but not science; music but not mathematics; pimping but not physics; entertainment but not economics? Who told you that you were naked?

It's time for brothers to show up and stand up. As God clothed Adam and Eve, God will cover our shame, our guilt, our insecurities, our failures, and our past. God will cover us with God's love, strength, peace, and grace.

Prayer: God bless and cover the men and boys in our lives and community. Strengthen them, hold them, and empower them now. In Jesus' name. Amen.

Created for Greatness

Read Psalm 8.

You've made them only slightly less than divine, crowning them with glory and grandeur. (Psalm 8:5)

This is a word for our young people. It is a reminder that you were created not for mediocrity but greatness. Take pride in who you are and whose you are. Traditional history books will never tell the whole story of our history and contributions to American society. But you need to know that you have the DNA of creative, spiritual, strong, and beautiful people. You got it going on. You are the bomb. You are off the chain. You are of value to God. You have all the right stuff and divine ingredients to excel, surpass, achieve, accomplish, and attain all God has for you, your life, and your future. When God created you, God did an exceptional, dynamite job. When God looked at you, God said, "That's very good."

My young sisters and brothers, embrace your dignity, embrace your uniqueness, and embrace your destiny. God created you to excel and not live below your potential. Don't ever be ashamed of who you are, how you look, your bold features, and your history. You were created in the image of God, which was God's way of placing a stamp of approval on your life. Embrace with pride and respect your uniqueness.

The operative word in your life should always be R-E-S-P-E-C-T. Carry yourself with respect. Dress with respect. Walk with respect. Talk with respect. Treat others with respect. And demand respect. You have been crowned with glory and honor, which means there is no room in your life for mediocrity or mediocre people. Don't trip over "haters"; be the one God created you to be. God created you for greatness. It's written all over you. Great things are coming out of you. Great things are in store for you. Live in to it and be it. You were created for greatness.

Prayer: Lord, pull out greatness in each of us, especially our young people. Remind them and us that you expect great things from us and out of us. We declare it done, in the name of the Great One, Jesus Christ. Amen.

From Dashed Hopes to Recovered Dreams

Read Luke 24:13-35.

They said to each other, "Weren't our hearts on fire when he spoke to us along the road and when he explained the scriptures for us?" (Luke 24:32)

We all know how it feels to have the rug of hope pulled from under us. We all know what it's like to have our dreams turn into nightmares of pain, hopelessness, and despair. We all know what it's like to have things not quite work out according to plan. That's what it must have been like for those two brothers on the road to Emmaus. They were trying to make sense of the tragic events of that weekend after the death of Jesus. When Jesus died, their dreams and hopes died with him. As they walked those long and lonely eight miles from Jerusalem to Emmaus, drowning in their pain, dashed hopes, and shattered dreams, Jesus showed up and began to walk with them.

Isn't that just like Jesus? He always shows up to walk with us as we journey on the road of our dashed hopes. He always intervenes in our situations and disrupts our stuff to help move us from despair to hope, from defeat to victory, and from displaced dreams to recovered dreams.

The promise is that we are never alone. On the road to Emmaus, those two brothers did not recognize Jesus. But when they came to the Lord's Table, Jesus' presence was made known. Jesus' presence restored their hopes, renewed their strength, and recovered their dreams. As those of the old-school church used to say, "He may not come when you want him, but he's always on time." We can make it and we can take whatever life throws at us if Jesus walks with us. Our slave ancestors would say, "I want Jesus to walk with me; I want Jesus to walk with me; all along my pilgrim journey; Lord, I want Jesus, to walk with me."

Prayer: Lord, walk with us and all whose hopes have been dashed by circumstances and help them and us recover dreams of plans you have for us. Today, Lord, walk and talk with us so that our hearts may burn with your presence. In your name we pray. Amen.

Divine Interruptions

Read Matthew 1:18-25.

*As he was thinking about this, an angel from the Lord appeared to him
in a dream and said, "Joseph son of David, don't be afraid to take
Mary as your wife, because the child she carries was conceived
by the Holy Spirit." (Matthew 1:20)*

Yesterday's Scripture and today's Scripture seem out of place for February, given that we celebrated Christmas just two months ago and Easter is yet to come. But like yesterday's Scripture, this story and Joseph's response to this divine interruption are timeless and fit in any season in our lives. We all have been privy to one of God's divine interruptions. Those interruptions can sometimes surprise us and knock us right off our feet. God can, at a moment's notice, intrude our space, interrupt our plans, rearrange our agendas, reroute our direction, and even alter our lives, causing us to reassess where we are and rethink where we want to go.

Joseph's encounter with God's divine interruptions changed his life, his plans, and his destiny. I have always liked this passage of Scripture because it says that Joseph was just as important in the birth of Jesus as was Mary. God chose him with deliberate care just as God had chosen Mary. With Mary's surprise pregnancy announcement, Joseph's plan was to end the relationship privately. But God had other plans.

We should always be on our toes when dealing with God because God will interrupt our routines. Just expect the unexpected. You have an appointment with destiny. You have a date with purpose. You have a scheduled rendezvous with greatness. Presently, things might look chaotic, out of control, crazy, out of reach, and a downright mess, but God can take that mess and transform it into a miracle. When God interrupts, it means God has other plans. Tell God to bring it on. You are ready for one of God's surprise interruptions because with God all things are possible.

Prayer: Lord, here we are. We're ready for a divine interruption. Take charge and take care as you lead us toward our destined place in life. Amen.

That Was Then, This Is Now

Read Galatians 1:11-24.

They only heard a report about me: "The man who used to harass us now preaches the faith that he once tried to destroy." (Galatians 1:23)

The only thing we know is inevitable in life is—change. Some change is good and some isn't. Some was planned, some unplanned. Some change brought us joy, some brought sorrow. We don't do change well because it requires that we think differently, see differently, interact differently, love others differently, and filter our perspectives differently. How we handle changes in life will determine how we move into God's new future prepared for us. There will always be those who will doubt and look suspiciously at the positive change that has been claimed.

That was the Apostle Paul's issue. He had experienced such a radical change through his encounter with Jesus Christ on that Damascus road that some were suspicious of his claims. All they knew is that the man who was once a feared persecutor of those who followed Christ was now preaching the gospel of Christ. Paul had to convince them: that was then, this is now.

The gospel of Christ is a change agent, and it won't leave us the way it found us. When the gospel infiltrates our lives, communities, politics, and churches, a change has to take place. The gospel can change structures, institutions, attitudes, minds, circumstances, and situations. It can change perspectives, people, destinies, and churches—and yes, it can change even us. We can never reach our full potential or our destined place in life if we are not willing to face and embrace the various changes God proposes for our lives. When the gospel gets hold of us we can look at our past and say "That was then," and we can look at ourselves in the present and say "This is now."

What's good about this is the changed then become change agents. Others need to know that they can experience the positive change we have experienced in Christ.

Prayer: Lord, help us become the changed, who ourselves become change agents for good in the world around us. Help us embrace the positive change that you are pouring into our lives today. In Jesus' name. Amen.

Storm Survivors

Read Luke 8:22-25.

Filled with awe and wonder, they said to each other, "Who is this? He commands even the winds and the water, and they obey him!" (Luke 8:25b)

In 2005, when Hurricane Katrina devastated the Gulf Coast, our church opened its doors to minister to many of the evacuees who came to the Dallas area from New Orleans. I still have vivid memories of an encounter I had with a woman who had spent time in the Superdome. We were feeding hundreds of persons in our Community Life Center. A woman from New Orleans was crying uncontrollably, grabbing my hand and holding it tightly all the while shaking her head and saying to me, "You just don't know what we saw." While I tried to console her, another brother from New Orleans put his hand on her shoulder and said, "Baby, we've been to hell and back but we will survive."

Many of us have been through some severe challenges and storms in our lives. We've literally been to hell and back, but we survived because of our faith in the God who would never leave us behind, but who stuck with us in the midst of it all. Our survival from past storms and those to come is dependent not on our physical strength, but on our spiritual fitness and preparedness. In this life, we must be ready for the unexpected.

When the disciples wake Jesus up in the middle of that storm, the Lord confidently and powerfully intervenes in the situation. The Lord put those destructive forces in their place. He rebuked the wind and the raging waters, bringing peace out of the chaos. What the Lord did for the disciples on the Sea of Galilee, the Lord will do for us when we encounter our rough seas and howling winds of life. You too will be as you have always been, a bona fide storm survivor.

Prayer: Lord, speak peace in the midst of our storms in life, society, and in the church. Your voice can calm raging waters and quiet strong winds. Today, Lord, we will live as the instruments of that peace. Amen.

Winners Don't Act Like Losers

Read Romans 8:31-39.

No, in all these things we are more than conquerors through him who loved us. (Romans 8:37 NRSV)

Everybody likes to root for a winner. Everybody wants to be on a winning team. And because of who we are and whose we are, we are winners. Because of the power that is at work in us, the Apostle Paul is encouraging us to stand in a spirit of bold defiance. Paul dares anything to bring it on because if God is for us, who or what can be against us? That's the attitude of winners who refuse to live and act like losers. We have the power to defy anything that possesses a threat to our spiritual well-being.

We can walk and live with the swagger and confidence of winners because Paul says, "We are more than conquerors." In order to describe who we are as winners, and the power we wield in Christ, Paul used a compound word because one word wasn't sufficient. "More than conquerors" translated means we are superior conquerors, top-notch champions, unequaled winners, and unrivaled victors. We are winners who refuse to act like losers. We are ultimate winners so we need not live like dismal losers, because greater is the one who is in you than the one who is in the world. Winners don't act like losers.

Whatever we are facing and whatever is facing us can be handled because we are more than conquerors. We will survive the suffering, the hurts, the disappointments, the opposition, the challenges, life's changes, the unpopular diagnosis, the unexpected, the sorrows, the tears, the breakups, the breakdowns, the ups, the downs. "What shall we say in response to these things?" This is how winners respond, "If God is for us, who can be against us?" We are part of a winning team and God's got the winning strategy. Now go out there and act and live like the winner you are.

Prayer: Lord, may any fear in my mind, my heart, or my life be released today. Empower me to live like the winner you intend me to be. Help us, Lord, to live as more than conquerors. In Jesus' name do we pray. Amen.

Walking with a Limp

Read Genesis 32:22-31.

**The sun rose as Jacob passed Penuel, limping because of his thigh.
(Genesis 32:31)**

All of us have stuff in our lives with which we struggle. We all learn how to walk with limps. That we may try to disguise them, over-look them, never discuss them, or ever acknowledge them does not negate the fact that they're still there. However, we'll never get our blessing out of them until we learn how to deal with them. Living with limps in our lives is not bad, scandalous, or contrary to our faith; it just means we've been through some things that left their mark on us.

Like Jacob, we have to wrestle with some stuff in order to confront it, and face it in order to get blessed through it. Jacob's struggle lasted all night long. It was intense, long, hard, and emotionally draining. He was in the battle for his sanity, life, and future. He struggled until he was injured and he came out a different man than he was when he went in. Jacob teaches us that we all can live positive, blessed, and faith-filled lives with a limp.

In order for God to get out of us what's already in us, we might have to go through some intense and even painful gut-wrenching wrestling matches with our stuff, our God, and ourselves. And it is through the struggle that we are transformed into credible witnesses of the faith. The struggle between Jacob and God did not destroy him; it trans-formed him. The limp would forever remind him of his new identity and how he got it.

When the sun came up, it shone upon a new man—a man with a limp. Blessed, but with a limp. Headed toward a new future, but with a limp. Limp into your destiny. Limp into your future. Limp into your healing. Hold on until you get your blessing.

Prayer: Lord, we are holding on to you in the struggle, and we won't let go until we get our blessing. We are willing to limp into our new day as long as you go with us. In Jesus' name. Amen.

Overcoming a Poolside Mentality

Read John 5:1-9.

When Jesus saw him lying there, knowing that he had already been there a long time, he asked him, "Do you want to get well?" (John 5:6)

Bitter and painful experiences have the potential to cripple us, scar us, and maim us, leaving us content with hanging around the pools of broken dreams, dashed hopes, dysfunctional relationships, unhealthy friendships, and destructive addictions. It is not God's will for us to live broken, crippled, or dysfunctional lives. But we have to have the will and desire to get up and leave behind our poolside mentality in order to go to where God is leading.

For thirty-eight years, the man in John 5 went to the same place, at the same time, hung out with the same people, and, unfortunately, ended up with the same results. He became comfortable hanging around at the pool and leaving the same way that he came. That is why he could not answer Jesus directly when asked if he wanted to be made well. He had grown accustomed to poolside living: a mentality where no one around the pool was getting healed or better; it was just a place to hang out and hope for the best. We can do better and the Lord is calling for better. We need to answer his question and do what he says.

It's time that we get up, change our environments, refuse to exist on excuses, and get out. It's time that we take charge and take care of business. We should never get used to living a crippled and dependent life; we should never get used to mediocrity and failure that requires a changed mind-set. Get up and get out and watch as relationships are healed, homes restored, churches revived, communities rebuilt, and dreams fulfilled. We can go where others once said we could not, and do what others said we could not. In the words of the African American spiritual, "I'm so glad Jesus lifted me; singing, glory hallelujah, Jesus lifted me!"

Prayer: Lord, raise us up out of our poolside mentalities. Help us get into situations that are good for us and away from those that are not good for us. Empower us to take up our beds and walk. In Jesus' name. Amen.

Touching the Untouchables

Read Mark 1:40-45.

A man with a skin disease approached Jesus, fell to his knees, and begged, "If you want, you can make me clean." (Mark 1:40)

Every human being is of sacred worth to God. Every human being is created in the image of God. One of the greatest saints in the church, Mother Teresa, said, "The dying, the crippled, the mentally ill, the unwanted, the unloved—they are Jesus in disguise." Her life was lived touching the untouchable. Jesus' whole ministry was built on his ability to attract and touch the unwanted in society. Regardless of their race, gender, culture, status, or class, Jesus reached out his hand and touched them with his love, his grace, and his mercy. He touched the saved and the unsaved, the faithful and the adulterer, the tax collector and the thief, the player and the pimp, the lady and the prostitute, the protector of life and the murderer, the law-abiding citizen and the ex-offender. Jesus was in the business of touching the untouchables.

To often we like to pick and choose whom we'll touch and from whom we'll keep away. We like to draw lines in the sand and make judgments based on which side of the line others or we land. We draw religious lines, denominational lines, racial lines, gender lines, cultural lines, political lines, theological lines, and economic lines. Jesus was in the habit, and so should we be, of touching the untouchables and those who needed to be reached with love, mercy, acceptance, and grace.

Jesus' compassion for the leper in Mark 1 moved him to act. Our compassion for others should move us to act. The touch of our hands should bring healing and not division. Our hands should embrace and not push away; they should hold and not oppress. Our touch can make all the difference in this world. It can restore dignity. It can restore lives. It can restore love. It can restore peace. Today, reach out and touch someone who has been labeled untouchable.

Prayer: Lord, may the touch of our hands bring the healing the world needs. Help us touch the untouchable as you have touched us. In Jesus' name. Amen.

How We Got Over . . .

Read Deuteronomy 7:7-9.

No, it is because the LORD loved you and because he kept the solemn pledge he swore to your ancestors that the LORD brought you out with a strong hand and saved you from the house of slavery, from the power of Pharaoh, Egypt's king. (Deuteronomy 7:8)

The African American story is one of struggle, inhumane treatment, segregation, lynching, Jim Crow, and substandard housing, but it also includes survival and victory. When reviewing our history, recall the lyrics of that old gospel song written by Clara Ward and sung by Mahalia Jackson: "My soul looks back and wonders how I got over." As we come to the close of the month that is officially known as Black History Month, we need to constantly remind ourselves and others daily from generation to generation, who we are and whose we are.

Africans in the diaspora have always related to Israel's story of enslavement, captivity, and liberation because it so much mirrored our history in this nation. And we knew God valued us and God invested in us. Because we knew who we were, many were on the front lines of justice, fighting for their dignity, their rights, their place, and their liberation.

History and experience have taught us God can be trusted. God has integrity. What God says God will do God will do. We are living off the promises God made to the ancestors, which is how we got over. And before we get it twisted, be it known that had it not been for the Lord who was on our side, we would have been wiped out a long time ago. We survived the door of no return. We survived being snatched from our homeland. We survived the Middle Passage. We survived slavery. We survived the Ku Klux Klan. We survived because we are not in this struggle alone.

Prayer: Lord, let us never forget what you have done for us historically as well as spiritually. Help us tell the story of how we got over by your mighty hand of power and grace. In Jesus' name do we pray. Amen.

Giant Slayers

Read 1 Samuel 17:33-47.

But David told the Philistine, "You are coming against me with sword, spear, and scimitar, but I come against you in the name of the LORD of heavenly forces, the God of Israel's army, the one you've insulted." (1 Samuel 17:45)

We've all had to learn how to face and deal with issues and persons who appeared larger and bigger than life. Maybe that is the reason the story of David and Goliath has intrigued, encouraged, and strengthened people down through the years. Modern-day giants feed on our fears and latch onto our anxieties while bullying us, taunting us, gnawing at us, and intimidating us trying to scare us into submission. Whatever appears to be gigantic in your life, you are a giant-slayer.

When David saw Goliath and then saw how his own people reacted, he couldn't believe it. He saw the same giant. He heard the same taunts. He heard the same challenge. He heard the same rebuke. He saw the same looming presence. But he still could not understand the fear. Why be afraid of this giant? The only thing about a giant that is true is the bigger they are, the harder they fall.

When confronted with your giants, refuse to be moved by fear, but instead be moved by faith because you are a giant-slayer. When mobilized by fear instead of faith we start coming up with all sorts of excuses for why we cannot overcome those looming presences in our lives. David knew what he saw, but also knew whom he served, the God of Israel. David, in the name of God, stood toe to toe with the giant.

When faced with the giants of oppression, sorrow, bad economic times, unemployment, relationships, people, trouble, trials, and tribulations, stand in the name of our God. Our power is in the name of the Lord. The battle that you face is not yours; it belongs to the Lord.

Prayer: Strengthen us, Lord, to stand up to our giants. Help us know that no matter how big they are, you are bigger. Through you, we are giant-slayers. In Jesus' name. Amen.

It's Just One of Those Days

Read Psalm 30.

LORD, my God, I cried out to you for help, and you healed me. (Psalm 30:2)

We all have had one of those days. A day when it seems nothing goes right. A day when it seems we're going backward and not forward. Days when relationships seem to be going awry, the highs are offset by the lows, success is undermined by failure, and our joys are numbed by our hurts. Those days when despair covers us, depression grips us, and despondency shadows us. That's when we shake our heads and say to ourselves, "It's just one of those days."

Unfortunately, we cannot control our external circumstances, but we can choose how we will respond. We can choose to sulk and have a pity party or we can look up and throw ourselves a praise party. The writer of Psalm 30 seems to have had his share of "those days," but it appears that instead of sitting in ashes and putting on sackcloth while feeling sorry for himself, he headed to the Temple and got his praise on. The psalmist had discovered that prayer and praise can get a person through just about anything. That's why the psalmist says, "I exalt you, LORD, because you pulled me up; you didn't let my enemies celebrate over me."

Too often we want a testimony without going through the test that produces it. No test. No testimony. When experiencing one of those days, encourage yourself by telling yourself that this is only a test; it did not come to stay but to pass. It is a temporary moment; it's a setup, because God is staging a dramatic and miraculous comeback.

One of those bad days will soon give way to God's new, bright day. Then we will discover that what we thought would break us, God used to make us. What we thought would destroy us, God used to build us. What we thought would weaken us, God used to strengthen us. And whatever the night stole from us, God will restore in the morning.

Prayer: God, help us through those days when we struggle to make sense of things. Help us hold on through the night experiences of life while having faith in knowing that your joy will meet us in the morning. Amen.

It Won't Be Like This Always

Read Luke 21:25-28.

"Now when these things begin to happen, stand up straight and raise your heads because your redemption is near." (Luke 21:28)

Our faith is one that constantly reminds us that God has not abandoned us to the horrors in the world, our communities, and our lives. We have something to look toward, to hope in, and long for that is better than what is now.

God has not given us over to the devices of evil plots and plans of destruction. God has better plans, bigger plans, better dreams, a greater purpose, and a more winnable strategy. God will win the debate and the struggle between good and evil. God will have the final word.

This is a call to live within the tension of the not yet and the present. We can't sit on the sidelines of life waiting for what will be. Jesus taught us to pray, "Your kingdom come. Your will be done, on earth as it is in heaven" (Matthew 6:10 NRSV). Whatever's going on in heaven, we ought to be living and working toward its fulfillment on earth. Day by day, as we look toward God's promised fulfillment, we are chipping away at those things that are not of God that are manifesting their demonic presence now. Our witness is dismantling Satan's kingdom bit by bit right now. We are called to chip away at sin. We are chipping away at injustice, racism, sexism, poverty, the effects of HIV, and the ravages of war. We are working toward God's goal, building God's kingdom brick by brick because our faith tells us it won't be like this always.

As we close out this month, the challenge is for us to continue to live faithfully with a sense of urgency, knowing we will be held accountable for how we've lived, what we've done, and who we've helped along the way. The Apostle Paul says in Galatians 6:9, "Let's not get tired of doing good, because in time we'll have a harvest if we don't give up." Keep it up because the struggle continues.

Prayer: Lord, keep us focused on the goals of the Kingdom while continuing to fight the fight of faith. Keep us moving toward your goals for the world and our lives because we know it won't be like this always. In Jesus' name. Amen.